This book belongs to the collection of

Share your colored versions with us ! We love seeing your results and hearing from you we are social !

The Official FB book page, stay on top of what we have in the works !
www.facebook.com/globaldoodlegems
The Community group, share your colored pages, meet the artists, enjoy exclusive freebies, take part in community Charity books and so much more......
www.facebook.com/groups/globaldoodlegems/
Follow us on Twitter.... @GlobalDoodlegem
We are on Instagram too
@globaldoodlegems for instagram
...and if you are not social like that we have a blog
globaldoodlegems.wordpress.com

Copyright © 2018 Global Doodle Gems
All rights are reserved by Global Doodle Gems.
Duplication of pages for personal use are allowed. You are invited to color the pages then scan/post your coloured versions to social networks, mentioning the book title and author/artist (Global Doodle Gems).
All artwork and images are protected by copyright laws. This book or any portion thereof may not, otherwise, be reproduced and/or distributed or transmitted without the express written permission of the artist/publisher of Global Doodle Gems.
All of us from the Global Doodle Gems wish you a colortastic time and look forward to seeing your wonderful color results online !

Never Too Many Hearts
The Big Fat Book
of
Heart Designs
These Heart Designs I made with Love and Valentines in Mind…
hopefully you will find them great for expressing your love…
or even dreaming of love !
The series of Designs consist of 3 types of Designs
This book contains all 3 books
1. Abstract Love
2. Lovely'Dala's
3. Love the patterns
I hope you will enjoy coloring these drawings of mine
and that they will help you relax and find inner peace
and joy with your colors !

I wish to thank
Johanna Ans and Manuela Bremer
from the buttom of my heart for their
lovely colorings for the cover art work !
Maria Wedel

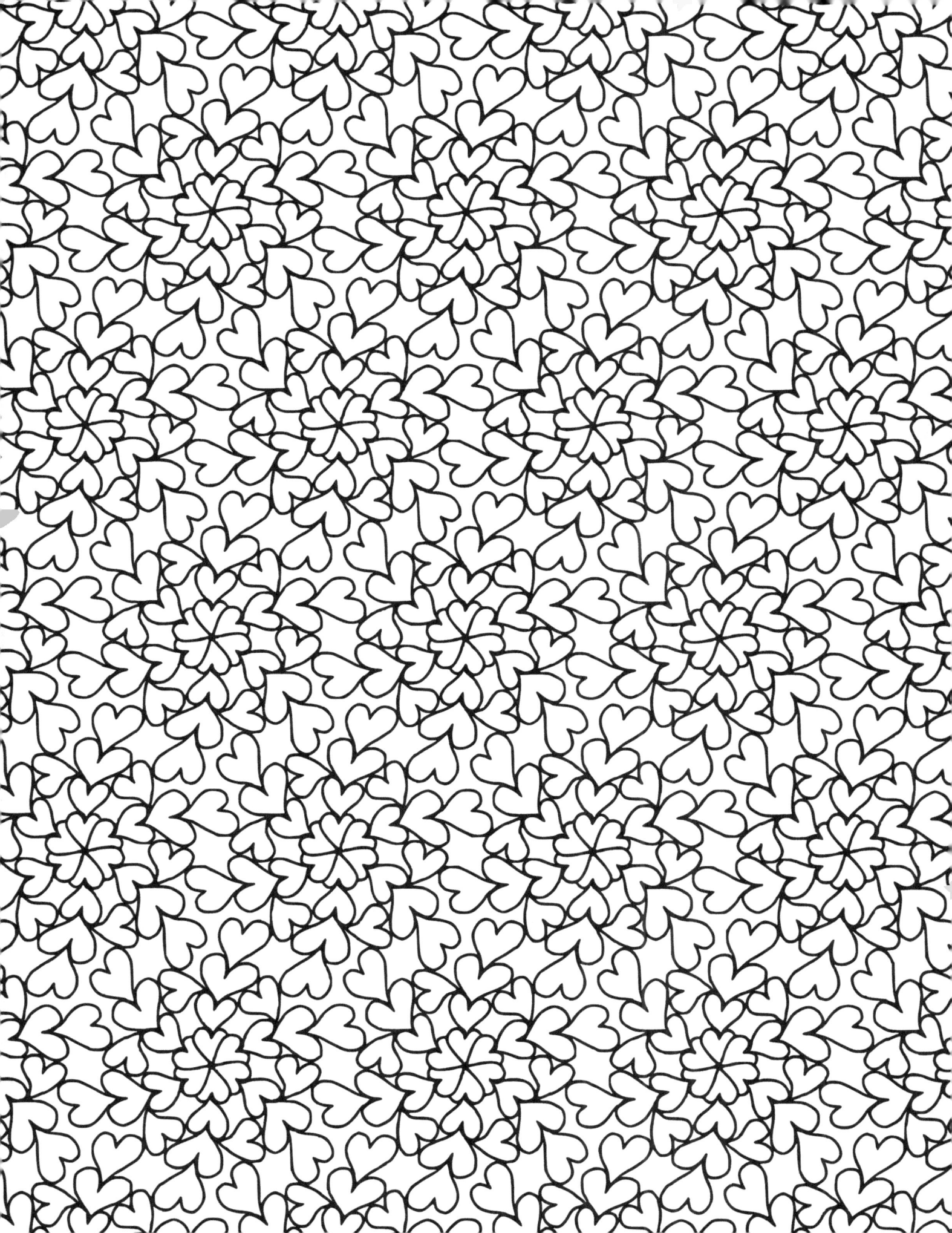

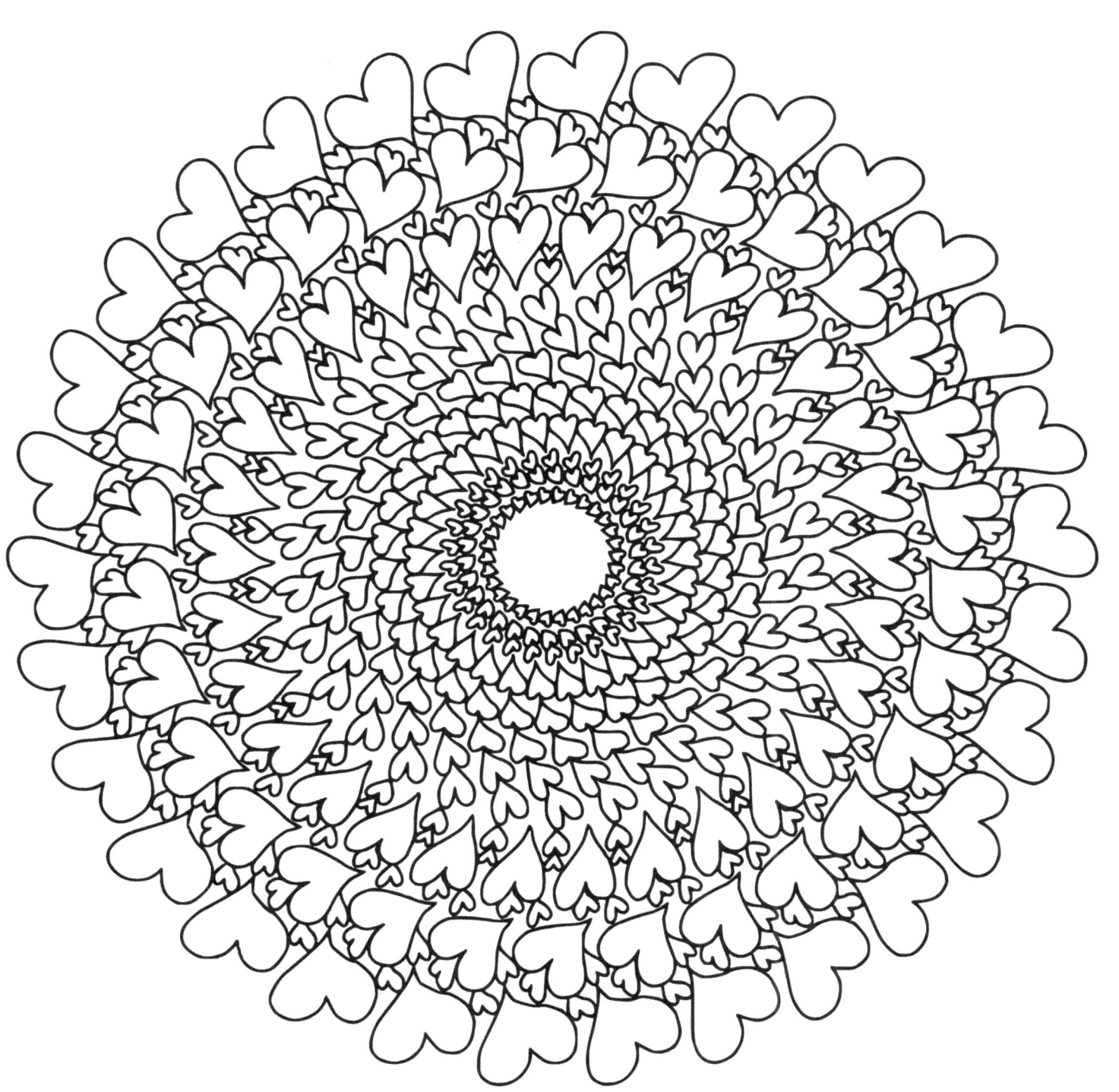

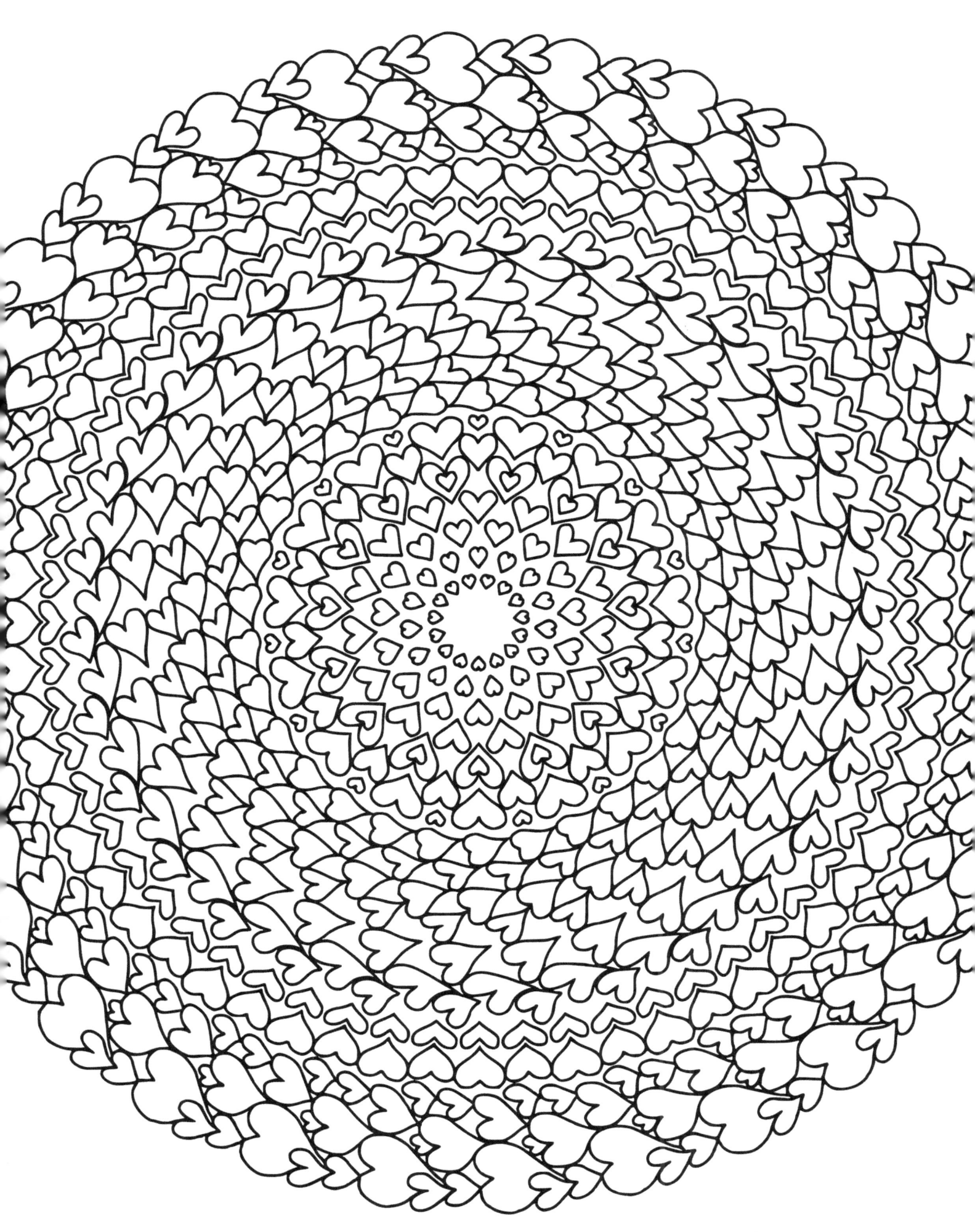

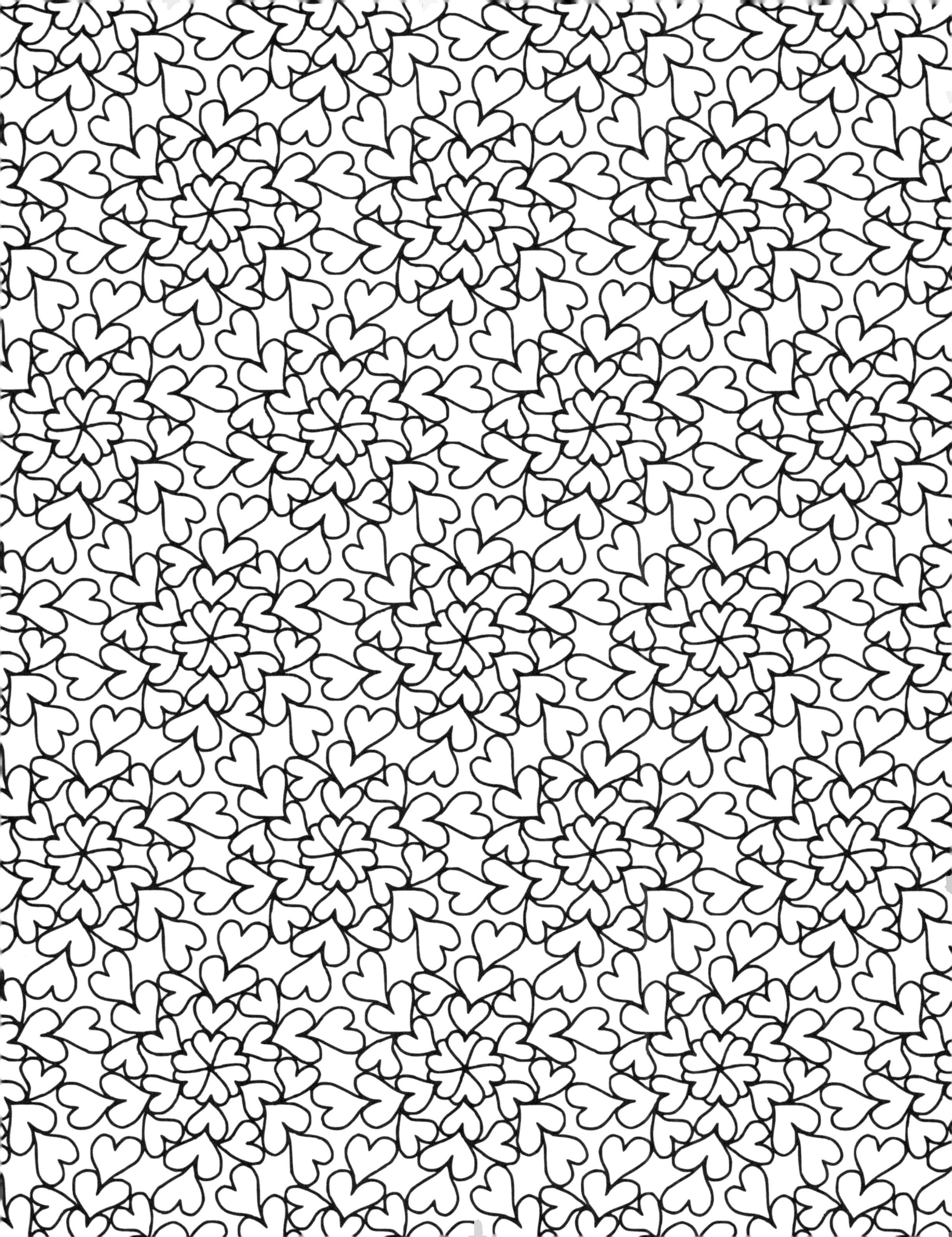

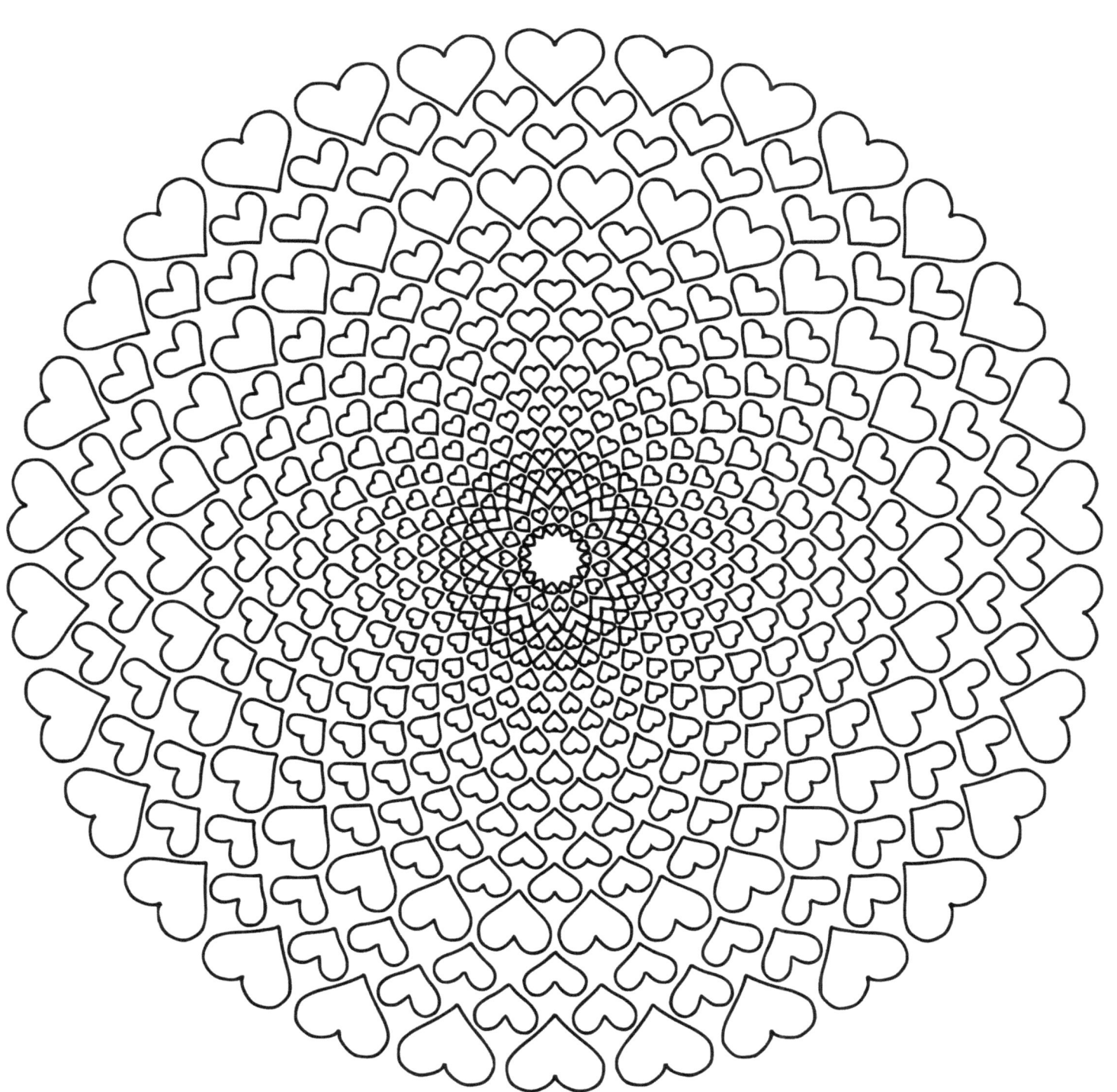

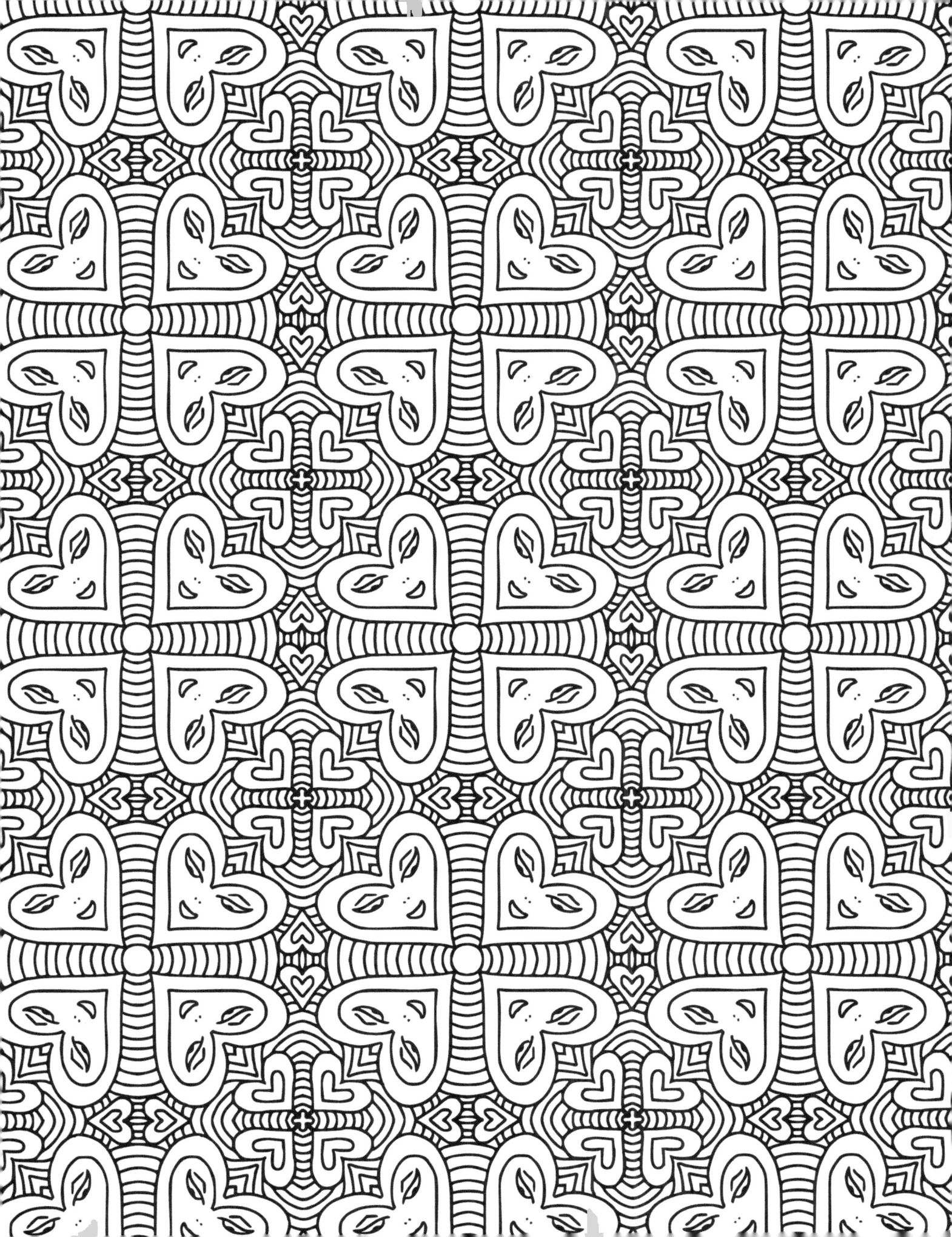

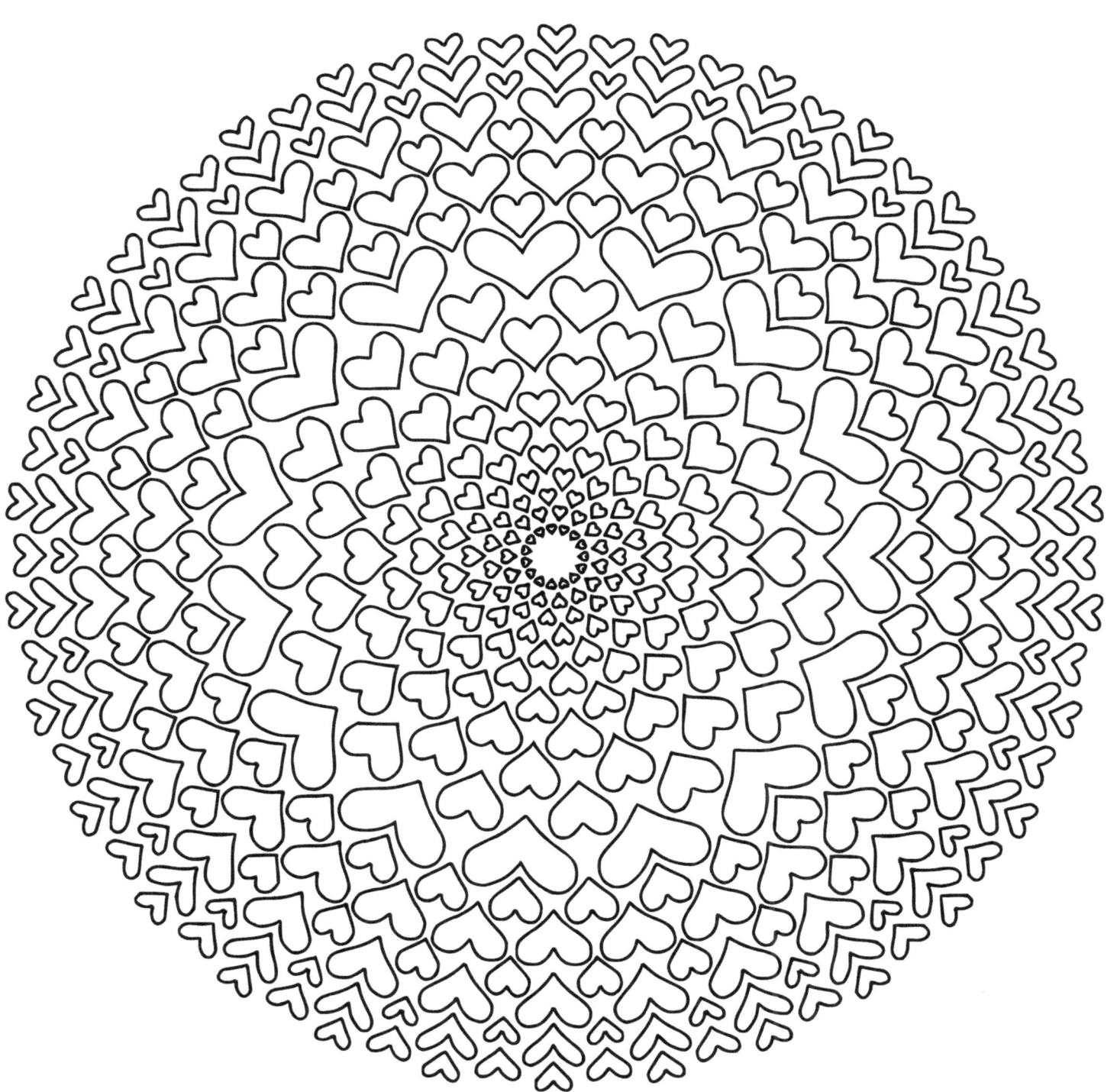

Test your colors here on the samples from
"My Pocket Coloring Companion"
&
"My Coloring Companion"

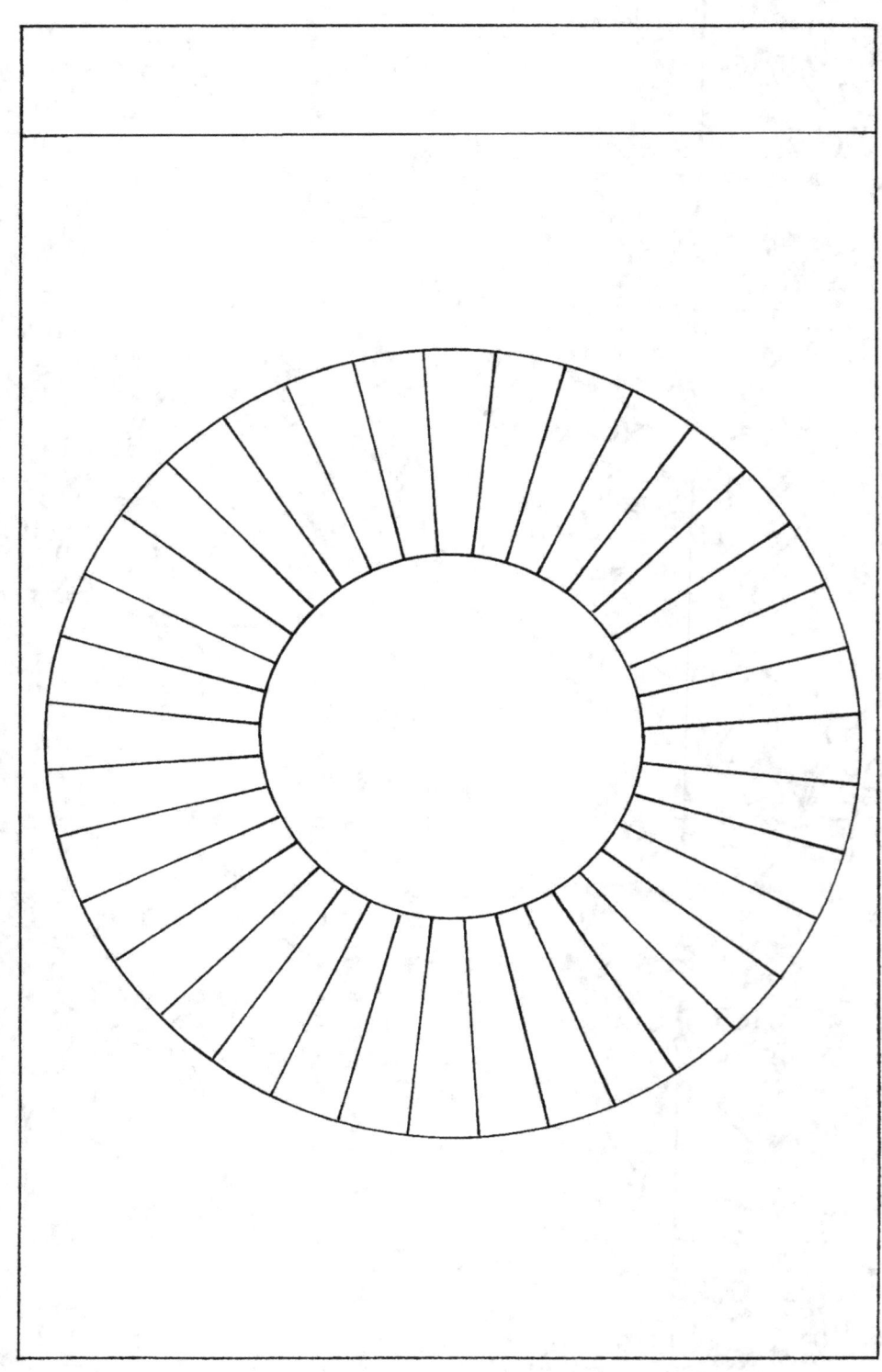

www.ingramcontent.com/pod-product-compliance
Lightning Source LLC
Chambersburg PA
CBHW082322220526
45470CB00008B/2373